UNDERSTANDING THE UNITED NATIONS

The Official Guidebook

Department of Public Information
United Nations, New York

Table of Contents

Welcome to the United Nations.

The "world Organization" is your Organization. Founded in 1945, it exists to help fulfil the aspirations of all the world's people for peace, justice and prosperity. Its Charter — an inspiring summons to global cooperation for the common good — is the legal and moral foundation of international relations.

Increasingly, our daily lives are lived in a global context. Challenges such as poverty, environmental degradation, injustice and crime affect us all, and the world public expects the world Organization to respond. This is as it should be. As the forum for all nations, the United Nations is uniquely placed to address today's complex problems.

But to succeed in the noble endeavour of international cooperation, your support is vital. I urge you to learn more about the purposes and principles of the United Nations. Working together, in this era of new opportunities, we can make a crucial difference in the common quest for development, peace and justice for the benefit of all humanity.

Kofi A. Annan
Secretary-General

INTRODUCTION

Ｎew York City, host to the United Nations, is noted for its dynamic and ever-changing skyline in its dramatic setting on Manhattan Island overlooking the East River. The dynamics of change have also resulted in the transformation and extraordinary growth of our world Organization since the signing of the United Nations Charter on 26 June 1945 by the 51 original Member States. Today, with membership in the United Nations having more than tripled, the view across the river of time presents a vastly different picture than most of us could have anticipated just a few years ago.

▾ *The flags of the UN Member States are raised each working day by UN Security Officers to fly in front of UN Headquarters in New York City.*

At no other time in its history has the United Nations been called upon to play so many vital roles or been so actively engaged. Recent years have witnessed impressive global progress towards democratic government, sustainable development, the observance of human rights and the peaceful settlement of disputes. The new climate of international cooperation has created fresh opportunities for the application of the Charter and the attainment of its goals.

The multidimensional work of the United Nations is channelled through its six principal organs: the General Assembly, the Security Council, the Economic and Social Council, the Trusteeship Council, the Secretariat and the International Court of Justice. All are based at United Nations Headquarters, with the exception of the Court, which is located at The Hague, Netherlands.

The UN System or "family" also includes the specialized agencies and other intergovernmental organizations with their own mandate and expertise in a specific area of human need, which work with the United Nations and each other through, among other things, the coordinating machinery of the Economic and Social Council. Their outreach is "hands-on", direct and practical, and touches people in every corner of our Earth.

◀ *The 39-storey glass-and-marble tower of the UN Secretariat building soars above a dish antenna, part of a satellite communications system linking UN Headquarters with its offices and operations overseas.*

▲ *The brilliantly coloured flags of the UN Member States in front of UN Headquarters serve to remind visitors of the nearly universal membership in the world Organization.*

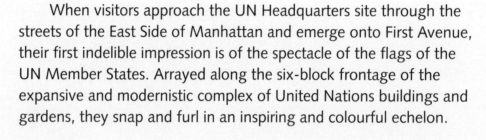

When visitors approach the UN Headquarters site through the streets of the East Side of Manhattan and emerge onto First Avenue, their first indelible impression is of the spectacle of the flags of the UN Member States. Arrayed along the six-block frontage of the expansive and modernistic complex of United Nations buildings and gardens, they snap and furl in an inspiring and colourful echelon.

In a few short steps the visitor passes, through the ornamental iron entry gates of the UN complex, from New York City into international territory. It is so designated by agreement with the United States of America, host country to the United Nations, to serve as common ground to all nations. The land for this unique establishment, once a parcel of well-used commercial and industrial properties, was donated in 1946 by the American financier-philanthropist, John D. Rockefeller, Jr. Additional property, easements and improvements were provided by New York City to consolidate an easily accessible and self-contained site of operations.

In the euphoric and optimistic period following the end of the Second World War, there was unbridled enthusiasm at the prospect of establishing an international facility of unprecedented architectural and functional excellence for the new organization. With a $65 million interest-free loan from the United States as working capital, a team

▼ A teacher directs her class through the gates of the Visitors' Entrance as they arrive for a tour of UN Headquarters.

◀ *A section of the General Assembly Public Lobby. At centre is the Foucault Pendulum, a gift of the Netherlands which, by its motion in the course of a day, gives visual proof of the rotation of the Earth on its axis.*

of eminent international architects was assembled in New York under the leadership of Wallace K. Harrison of the United States. Known as the UN Headquarters Board of Design, it included such renowned architects of their day as N.D. Bassov (Soviet Union), Gaston Brunfaut (Belgium), Ernest Cormier (Canada), Le Corbusier (France), Liang Seu-Cheung (China), Sven Merkelius (Sweden), Oscar Niemayer (Brazil), Howard Robertson (United Kingdom), G.A. Soilleux (Australia) and Julio Vilamajo (Uruguay).

The three principal structures to emerge from their deliberations and innovative designs were the sweeping domed General Assembly Building, the towering 39-storey glass-and-marble Secretariat Building, and the rectangular Conference Building set along the East River. In 1961, the Ford Foundation provided a gift of $6.6 million for the addition of the Dag Hammarskjöld Library at the south-west corner of the site. The inspired design of the overall complex has stood the test of time and has proven to be an architectural, aesthetic and functional success in its service to the international community. The Organization has, however, outgrown its original accommodations and now occupies a few other office buildings in the immediate neighbourhood.

Over the years, UN Member States have generously endowed the Headquarters buildings and gardens with a collection of artworks and sculptures. Organizations and individuals have also provided a rich variety of trees, shrubs, plants and flowers for the gardens that provide a welcome green haven in one of the world's busiest and most densely populated cities.

While Headquarters is the hub of the Organization and a major centre of international diplomacy, United Nations staff are at work in all parts of the world. Their tasks are as diverse and urgent as the full range of critical issues which confront the global human family today.

◀ *A group of young Japanese tourists receives a briefing on the Headquarters complex from a UN Tour Guide.*

THE GENERAL ASSEMBLY

Sometimes described as the "Parliament of Nations", the General Assembly is the primary deliberative body of the United Nations. It convenes in its grand forum, the General Assembly Hall at United Nations Headquarters in New York, in plenary session from mid-September to mid-December every year, but it can also decide to meet in special or emergency sessions when necessary. When the Assembly is not in session, its work goes on in special committees and bodies.

More than 1,100 delegates and advisers can be accommodated in the rows of green leather-covered desks beneath the Assembly Hall's huge dome. All UN Member States are represented and each has one vote. Decisions on matters such as peace and security, budgets and admission of new members, require a two-thirds majority. Decisions on other questions are reached by simple majority.

The General Assembly has the right to discuss and make recommendations on all matters of concern to the Organization. It has no power to compel action by any government, but its recommendations carry the weight of world opinion. The President of the General Assembly, elected each year by the delegates, presides over the proceedings.

◄◄ *Nelson Mandela addressing the Special Committee against Apartheid on 24 September 1993. In April 1994, the United Nations coordinated the international observation of elections in South Africa in which Mr. Mandela was elected President, establishing a non-racial democratic government following decades of apartheid. On the podium behind him are (left to right):General Assembly President, S.R. Insanally of Guyana; Committee Chairman, Ibrahim A Gambari of Nigeria; and UN Secretary-General, Boutros Boutros-Ghali.*

▼*Delegates in the General Assembly.*

▸▸ *A general view of a plenary session of the General Assembly.*

Humankind uses thousands of languages and dialects in spoken communications and UN delegates speak to each other in many of these tongues. But to facilitate communication, the United Nations uses only six official languages: Arabic, Chinese, English, French, Russian and Spanish.

The first session of the General Assembly, attended by representatives of the 51 original Member States, was opened on 10 January 1946 at Central Hall, London. Nearly half a century later, following the great wave of decolonization and other dramatic changes on the international scene, 185 States now use the unique forum of the General Assembly as the premier vehicle for dialogue and consensus among nations, for facilitating international agreements, and for resolving global problems that are beyond the control of any one State.

▲ *A moment of silent prayer or meditation is traditionally observed by delegates at the opening of each annual session of the General Assembly.*

◀◀ *Conference Officers prepare the speakers list.*

◀ *Verbatim Reporters transcribe the complete spoken proceedings of each meeting.*

The technical work behind the scenes of each General Assembly meeting is diverse and highly specialized.

▲ *Technicians install a video "teleprompter" on the speakers rostrum to assist in the delivery of a speech by a visiting Head of State.*

▶ *A Simultaneous Interpreter in her glass-enclosed booth overlooking the General Assembly Hall.*

▲ *In recognition of the 50th anniversary of the United Nations, more than
130 Heads of State or Government and other world leaders assembled at UN
Headquarters from 22 to 24 October 1995 for a special commemorative meeting
of the General Assembly – the largest such gathering in history. At the end of the
meeting, the Assembly adopted a declaration reaffirming the purposes and
principles enshrined in the Organization's Charter.*

THE SECURITY COUNCIL

T he Security Council has primary responsibility under the Charter for the maintenance of international peace and security. The Council has 15 members: five permanent members – China, France, the Russian Federation, the United Kingdom of Great Britain and Northern Ireland, and the United States of America – and ten members elected by the General Assembly for two-year terms. Decisions on procedural matters require at least nine affirmative votes. Decisions on substantive questions require nine votes including the concurring votes of all five permanent members. This is the rule of "great Power unanimity", known more popularly as the "veto" power.

When a threat to peace is brought before the Council, it usually first asks the parties to reach agreement by peaceful means. The Council may also undertake mediation, set forth principles for a settlement or request the Secretary-General to investigate and report on a situation. If fighting breaks out, the Council tries to secure a cease-fire. It has the power to enforce its decisions by ordering economic sanctions (such as trade embargoes) or collective military action. The Council also sends peace-keeping forces (observers or troops) to troubled areas to help reduce tensions, keep opposing forces apart and create conditions under which peaceful solutions may be sought.

▲ *Peace-keeping troops from the UN Observer Group in Central America (ONUCA) destroy weapons surrendered voluntarily by Nicaraguan resistance forces in Yamales - El Paraíso, Honduras in April 1990, as part of the overall UN-aided peace process.*

◀◀ *The first summit-level meeting of the UN Security Council was held in January 1992. Attended by 13 Heads of State and Government and two Foreign Ministers, representing the 15 members of the Security Council, and by Secretary-General Boutros Boutros-Ghali, the meeting reaffirmed the Council's role in maintaining peace and security as originally envisioned in the UN Charter.*

▲ *A Kenyan soldier serving with the UN peace-keeping operation in the former Yugoslavia.*

In early 1997, 25,600 UN peace-keepers and observers provided by 71 countries were deployed in various parts of the world, such as Angola, Cyprus, Georgia, Haiti, Kashmir (India-Pakistan), Iraq-Kuwait, Liberia, the Middle East, Tajikistan, Western Sahara and the former Yugoslavia. Since 1948, more than 750,000 people, mostly military personnel but also civilians, have served with United Nations forces, and more than 1,400 peace-keepers have given their lives in service to the world community.

The Security Council also makes recommendations to the General Assembly on a candidate for Secretary-General, and on the admission of new Members to the United Nations. Together with the General Assembly, it elects the Judges of the International Court of Justice. While other organs of the United Nations make recommendations to Governments, the Council alone has the power to take decisions which Member States are obligated under the Charter to implement.

◀ A general view of the Security Council in session as voting takes place. The chamber and its furnishings were a gift of Norway and were designed by Arnstein Arnenberg. A mural, by Per Krogh, depicts humankind's effort to rise as a phoenix from the darkness of war and oppression to a better future.

▶ The UN flag is unfurled during the ceremony in Port-au-Prince, Haiti, on 31 March 1995, marking the transfer of command from the Multinational Force to the UN Mission in Haiti (UNMIH). At the end of 1996, the mission consisted of some 1,550 troops and civilian police from nine countries, with Canada, Pakistan, France, Mali and the United States the leading contributors to the Force.

▶ *Finnish peace-keeping troops with the UN Transition Assistance Group in Namibia (UNTAG) disembark from a military transport plane. In 1989, more than 8,000 military, police and civilian personnel of 120 nationalities monitored the Namibian electoral process.*

▼ *A Canadian medic with the UN Transitional Authority in Cambodia (UNTAC) examines an ailing child in a village near Phnom Penh in 1993. UN peace-keepers routinely provide such humanitarian assistance to local people in their areas of operation.*

▲ *Bulldozers destroying Iraqi SCUD ballistic missiles under the supervision of a UN inspection team at Al Taji military camp in Baghdad, Iraq.*

◄ *Swedish peace-keeping troops of Nordic Battalion 2, on duty in Bosnia and Herzegovina, assemble around an officer for a briefing on their assignment with the UN Protection Force (UNPROFOR).*

THE **E**CONOMIC AND **S**OCIAL **C**OUNCIL

The Economic and Social Council was established by the Charter as the principal organ to coordinate the economic and social work of the United Nations and its specialized agencies, programmes and institutions.

The Council has 54 members, who serve for three-year terms. Voting is by simple majority and each member has one vote. It holds one month-long session each year, alternating between New York and Geneva. The year-round work of the Council is carried out in its subsidiary bodies – committees and commissions – which meet at regular intervals and report back to the Council.

The subsidiary machinery of the Council includes:
- nine functional commissions (on social development, crime prevention and criminal justice, human rights, narcotic drugs, science and technology for development, sustainable development, the status of women, population and development, and statistics);
- five regional commissions (for Africa, Asia and the Pacific, Europe, Latin America and the Caribbean, and Western Asia);
- four standing committees and a number of standing expert bodies.

◀◀ *The Economic and Social Council in session. The Council chamber was designed by Sven Merkelius of Sweden, whose Government and people donated the furnishings.*

▸▸ Pre-natal care is available for a pregnant woman in this community clinic in Sierra Leone run by the UN Children's Fund (UNICEF). Such primary health care has significantly reduced infant mortality. The UN Population Fund (UNFPA) also invests heavily in maternal and child care and family planning.

▾ The Handpump Factory in Tempoal, on the east coast of Mexico, is a project designed by the UN Development Fund for Women (UNIFEM) to increase the earning power of rural women. The women successfully manufacture and install the pumps in rural communities which lack water systems.

The Council, among its many responsibilities, recommends and directs activities aimed at promoting economic and social development in developing countries by administering UN-assistance programmes, promoting observance of human rights, ending discrimination against minorities, spreading the benefits of science and technology, and fostering cooperation globally in such diverse areas as agriculture, health, labour, education, environment, social welfare, communications, drug abuse control, prevention of crime and treatment of offenders, housing and family planning, to mention just a few.

The Economic and Social Council also recognizes that non-governmental organizations active within areas of the Council's competence should have the opportunity to express their views. Some 1,500 non-governmental organizations possessing special experience, expertise and technical competence of value to the Council have consultative status, enabling them to send observers to public meetings of the Council and its subsidiary bodies and to submit written statements relevant to the Council's work.

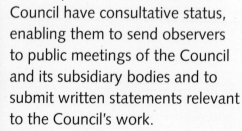

▸ *A young student in Mauritania. Nearly one billion adults in the world are illiterate; of these, 600 million are women. The global literacy campaign is led by the UN Educational, Scientific and Cultural Organization (UNESCO).*

▲ *The Government of Argentina and the UN Development Programme (UNDP) in April 1995 approved an innovative US$195 million project to improve on-the-job training to 100,000 youths. This young woman is learning to install reinforcing frames for concrete columns on a construction site in her neighbourhood in Mendoza. UNDP is the world's largest multilateral source of grant funding for development cooperation.*

◂ *Children in a flood-prone slum area of Dakka, Bangladesh, shiver in the monsoon rain which has driven them from their homes. UN agencies provide emergency disaster relief to the victims of such natural calamities, which afflict millions in developing countries.*

◄ *A new highway under construction in Papua New Guinea. The UN Environment Programme (UNEP) and other UN bodies seek to help nations integrate environmental and developmental concerns to achieve "sustainable development" – development which meets the needs of the present without compromising the ability of future generations to meet their own needs.*
In this way, industrialized and developing countries alike can utilize their natural resources and realize the benefits of development while maintaining and preserving their ecosystems.

▲ *The UN High Commissioner for Refugees (UNHCR) and other specialized agencies provide basic humanitarian care for millions of refugees and displaced persons throughout the world each day. Most are innocent victims of ethnic conflicts, civil wars, national confrontations and natural disasters.*

▸ *A group of 500 refugees who sought voluntary repatriation from India to Sri Lanka, from which they had originally fled, mostly in 1990, to escape violence. The UN High Commissioner for Refugees assisted in their return home and set up this reception centre at Talaimannar railway station, Mannar Island, from which the returnees were moved on to their home villages or were resettled in other areas of Sri Lanka.*

In an exodus of unprecedented scale and tragic consequence, hundreds of thousands of Rwandese refugees fled the political and ethnic violence afflicting their country in 1994, seeking refuge in neighbouring countries and assistance from the United Nations and international aid agencies. Some sought temporary shelter under blue tarpaulins provided, together with food and other relief supplies, by the UN High Commissioner for Refugees in Ntamba Camp in Muyinga Province, Northern Burundi.

THE TRUSTEESHIP COUNCIL

U nder the Charter of the United Nations, the International Trusteeship System was established to supervise the administration of Trust Territories placed under it by individual agreements with the States administering them. The basic objective of the System was to promote the political, economic and social advancement of the Trust Territories and their progressive development towards self-determination. The System applied to:

- Territories then held under mandates established by the League of Nations after the First World War;
- Territories detached from enemy States as a result of the Second World War;
- Territories voluntarily placed under the System by States responsible for their administration.

The aims of the Trusteeship System have been fulfilled to such an extent that all Trust Territories have attained self-government or independence, either as separate States or by joining neighbouring independent countries. The United Nations Trusteeship Agreement for the last of the original 11 Trusteeships– the Trust Territory of the Pacific Islands (Palau), administered by the United States of America –was terminated by the Security Council in November 1994. The Trusteeship Council, by amending its rules of procedure, will now meet as and where occasion may require.

◄◄ *The Trusteeship Council chamber was designed by architect Finn Juhl of Denmark, whose Government and people donated the furnishings. The statue on the far wall is carved from teak wood by Danish sculptor Henrik Starcke.*

The Original UN Trust Territories

- *British Togoland*
- *Somaliland*
- *French Togoland*
- *French Cameroons*
- *British Cameroons*
- *Tanganyika*
- *Ruanda-Urundi*
- *Western Samoa*
- *Nauru*
- *New Guinea*
- *Trust Territory of the Pacific Islands (Micronesia)*

Namibia (formerly South West Africa) was the only one of the seven African Territories once held under the League of Nations Mandate System that was not placed under the UN Trusteeship System. Instead, this vast and rich territory was held under the League of Nations mandate by South Africa until 1966, when the mandate was revoked by the United Nations.

The United Nations Council for Namibia was then established as the legal administering authority until the Territory became independent. After many years of complex and difficult negotiations, South Africa's withdrawal was closely followed by the achievement of Namibia's independence through free and fair elections held in 1989 under the supervision and control of the United Nations Transition Assistance Group (UNTAG). In April 1990, Namibia became the 160th Member State of the United Nations.

◀ Namibian children joyfully
display UNTAG bumper
stickers, which proclaim "Free
and Fair Elections" in the
Afrikaans language.

The decolonization efforts of the United Nations have as their guiding principal the "equal rights and self-determination of peoples" and devotion to the interests of dependent peoples as expressed in the Charter. Since 1960, the United Nations has also been directed by the General Assembly's Declaration on the Granting of Independence to Colonial Countries and Peoples. The Declaration's goal has been largely fulfilled. When the United Nations was founded in 1945, more than 750 million people – almost a third of the world's population – were living in Territories that were non-self-governing and dependent on colonial Powers. Since then, more than 80 nations formerly under colonial rule have become sovereign and independent and joined the United Nations as Member States.

As significant as are these achievements, and even with the success of the UN Trusteeship System after 30 years of concerted effort, some 2 million people in non-self-governing territories, mainly the populations of islands in the Caribbean and the Pacific, are still awaiting their opportunity to exercise their right to self-determination.

◀ *Two prospective voters, Herero women in their traditional dress, pose beneath a colourful sign urging Namibians to register to participate in the electoral process.*

THE INTERNATIONAL COURT OF JUSTICE

Also known as the World Court, the International Court of Justice is the principal judicial organ of the United Nations, and its Statute is an integral part of the UN Charter. The Court's role is to settle, in accordance with international law, the legal disputes submitted to it by States and duly authorized international organs and agencies. The submission of States to the Court's jurisdiction is based upon their consent. The Court is not open to private individuals.

The seat of the Court is at The Hague, Netherlands, and its official languages are English and French. The Court is composed of 15 Judges elected by the General Assembly and the Security Council for an eight-year term, for which they may stand for reelection. They are chosen on the basis of their judicial qualifications, not on the basis of nationality; however, no two Judges can be of the same nationality. Elections are held every three years for one third of the seats.

The cases submitted to the Court have covered a wide range of topics, including questions of land frontiers and maritime boundaries, territorial sovereignty, the non-use of force, non-interference in the internal affairs of States, diplomatic relations, hostage-taking, the right of asylum, nationality, guardianship, rights of passage and economic rights. Beyond the application of international law, the Court also plays an important role in its interpretation and development.

▲ *Many of the cases heard by the International Court of Justice have involved the Law of the Sea, particularly those provisions of the law related to maritime boundaries and fisheries.*

▸ *The 15 Judges and the
Registrar of the International
Court of Justice photographed
in the Peace Palace at
the Hague, Netherlands.
In 1995, the General
Assembly and the Security
Council filled a vacancy
on the Court by electing
Ms. Rosalyn Higgins (United
Kingdom) the first woman
Judge in the Court's history.*

▲ *Justices meet informally in their consultation chamber to discuss cases on their agenda.*

◀ *A lawyer presents his nation's case to the assembled justices in the Great Hall of the International Court of Justice. Only States may bring their cases before the Court.*

THE **S**ECRETARIAT

The Secretariat of the United Nations is the administrative and service arm of the Organization. Its chief administrative officer is the Secretary-General, who is appointed by the General Assembly, on the recommendation of the Security Council, for a five-year term. The present Secretary-General is Kofi Annan, of Ghana, who began his term of office in January 1997. His predecessors were (from left to right below):

Trygve Lie, of Norway, 1945-1953
Dag Hammarskjöld, of Sweden, 1953-1961
U Thant, of Burma (now Myanmar), 1961-1971
Kurt Waldheim, of Austria, 1972-1981
Javier Pérez de Cuéllar, of Peru, 1982-1991
Boutros Boutros-Ghali, of Egypt, 1992-1996

It was Mr. Trygve Lie, the first UN Secretary-General, who, at the end of his term of office, described this unique and demanding international post as "the most impossible job in the world". The Charter empowers the Secretary-General to bring to the attention of the Security Council any matter which threatens international peace and security and to provide "good offices" to help resolve international disputes. It is a task of enormous complexity and sensitivity in which the Secretary-General stands in the full glare of constant publicity before the international community. The Secretary-General is the embodiment of the Organization and must answer for its effectiveness.

Each Secretary-General also defines the job within the context of his particular day and age. In 1992, for example, at the request of the Security Council, Secretary-General Boutros-Ghali prepared "An Agenda for Peace", a far-reaching proposal for effective peace-keeping, peace-building and preventive diplomacy in the post-cold-war world. A complementary report – "An Agenda for Development" – was issued in 1994 in which the Secretary-General offered a blueprint for a re-energized drive to improve the human condition.

The Secretariat, an international civil service of more than 8,500 men and women from more than 170 countries, carries out the day-to-day work of the United Nations. These international civil servants take an oath not to seek or receive instructions from any Government or outside authority; rather, they and the Secretary-General answer to the United Nations for their activities. The work of the Secretariat includes servicing the other organs of the United Nations, administering peace-keeping operations and development programmes, organizing international conferences, surveying world economic and social trends, preparing studies on subjects such as human rights and disarmament, servicing conferences and meetings with interpretation and translation services, and providing electoral assistance to countries which request UN help in the process of democratization.

▾ *UN Security Officers are briefed on their day's duty roster at a morning muster in the General Assembly Lobby.*

The Map Room of the Dag Hammarskjöld Library contains about 70,000 maps and a library of atlases, gazetteers, guides and other reference works in many languages.

▲ The Central Reference Desk in the main Reading Room.

◄ The Woodrow Wilson Reading Room houses an important collection of books and documents dealing with the League of Nations and with international relations during the period between the two world wars. The collection was presented to the United Nations by the Woodrow Wilson Foundation.

▸A French Interpreter
in his booth in the
General Assembly Hall.

◀ *Night view of UN Headquarters, including the Secretariat, Dag Hammarskjöld Library (foreground) and General Assembly Building (centre).*

A TOUR OF THE UN

▶ *"Triumph of Peace",*
a mural tapestry depicting the
themes of Peace, Prosperity
and Equality, was designed by
Peter Colfe and was a gift of
Belgium. One of the largest
tapestries ever woven, the
piece is the work of 14 Belgian
artisans, who used 94,000
miles of yarn to create it. The
tapestry hangs prominently in
the Delegates Lobby of the
General Assembly Building.

Guided tours of UN Headquarters include an explanation of the aims, structure and activities of the Organization as well as a description of the works of art and architectural features along the tour route. Since 1952, some 35 million visitors from around the world have taken the tours, which are conducted daily by an international staff who, together, speak more than 20 languages.

Justly proud of their sparkling new Headquarters on the banks of the East River in New York City when it opened for occupancy in 1952, UN Member States immediately sought to embellish the meeting chambers, concourse and corridor walls, public spaces and gardens with numerous gifts of art. The practice has continued over the years as new nations have been admitted to UN Membership. Today, the UN complex houses an extraordinary multi-cultural collection of paintings, tapestries, artifacts and sculptures which enliven and beautify the buildings and gardens for the pleasure of visitors, diplomats and UN staff alike.

▼ *A knot in the barrel of a pistol is sculptor Kare Fredrik Reutersward's commentary on the folly of war and weapons. The bronze sculpture entitled "Non-Violence", was a gift of Luxembourg to the United Nations and is a popular attraction and photo opportunity for visitors to UN Headquarters.*

▶ *This mosaic mural entitled
"The Golden Rule" (Do unto
others as you would have
them do unto you) was
executed by the group of
Italian artisans known as
Cooperative Venetian Artistic
Mosaic, from a painting by
American artist Norman
Rockwell, and was a gift of the
United States of America.*

◀ *A stained-glass window by the French artist Marc Chagall depicts the themes of "Peace and Humankind". It was donated by the artist and UN staff members as a memorial to Secretary-General Dag Hammarskjöld of Sweden and others who died while on a peace mission in Africa in 1961. The window is located in the General Assembly Public Lobby.*

▶ Exquisitely carved by an
anonymous Indonesian
master, this elegant figure of a
Balinese Pedanda (Priest) in
solemn meditation represents
"Peace." It is made from
precious Bentawas satinwood
and was a gift of Indonesia.

◀ "Femme sur l'échelle"
(Woman on a Ladder), a
tapestry based on a painting
by Pablo Picasso, hangs in an
ante-room of the Security
Council.

▶ Spanning a 20-metre wall of
the Conference Building, this
mural by the Spanish artist
José Vela Zanetti was executed
"in situ" and depicts
humankind's epic struggle to
build a lasting peace.
The mural was donated
in 1952 by the Simon
Guggenheim Foundation.

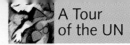

◀ *"Kiswa," a black silk prayer mantle embroidered in silver and gold, was a gift of Saudi Arabia. It was formerly hung in sacred tradition as a curtain across the portal of the Holy Kaaba in Mecca.*
In the foreground is a bronze sculpture by Marta Minjún, entitled "Reassembling History Towards Posterity", a gift of Argentina.

▼ *"Reclining Figure," a bronze sculpture by the British artist Henry Moore, graces the garden in the forecourt of the UN Secretariat Building. The piece was a gift of the Henry Moore Foundation.*

THE U.N GARDENS

▸ *Tour Guides in the UN garden.*

The United Nations gardens cover an area of some 327,000 square feet, attractively set out overlooking the East River to the North of the Headquarters complex. The original sycamores, pin oaks, sweet gums and honey locusts, mere saplings when the raw site was landscaped in 1952, are now mature and luxurious trees in their rows and groves. Thick hawthorn hedges, espaliered fruit trees and Japanese flowering cherry trees also border many of the walks and paths between lush beds of daffodils, roses and a brilliant variety of other flowers and shrubs, most of them donated by groups or individuals. A variety of sculptures from many nations, some of heroic proportions, provides another dramatic attraction.

The riverside promenade also offers a spectacular view of the broad East River estuary, framed by its large bridges and busy with constant ship traffic. During regular business hours and on weekends, the gardens are open to UN visitors and New Yorkers for whom it is a popular year-round refuge.

▾ *The massive sculpture entitled "Good Defeats Evil," by Zurab Tsereteli, of Georgia, depicts St. George slaying the dragon. A gift of the USSR and also known as the "Dragon of War", it is assembled from pieces of Soviet SS-20 and American Pershing nuclear missiles, which were destroyed under the terms of the Intermediate-Range Nuclear Forces Treaty of 1987 between the USA and the USSR.*

▴ *A family enjoys a walk through the rose garden at UN Headquarters. In the background, the Queensborough Bridge linking Manhattan Island with the borough of Queens rises over the East River. Also in the background is the bronze sculpture by Russian sculptor Evgeny Vuchetich, entitled "Let Us Beat Our Swords into Plowshares".*

▸ *The stainless steel sculpture entitled "Roots and Ties for Peace" by Yolanda d'Augsburg Ulm was given to the United Nations by the Brazilian Government in 1983.*

◄ *The graceful structure of the Japanese Peace Bell. Contributions of coins by children of 60 nations and various kinds of metal were used to cast the bell, which is housed in a structure made of Japanese cypress wood. The bell was donated by the United Nations Association of Japan in 1954.*

THE **UN**ITED NATIONS
POSTAL **AD**MINISTRATION

The United Nations is the only organization in the world, other than a nation or Territory, which has the privilege of issuing its own postage stamps. The establishment of the UN Postal Administration was made possible by an agreement between the United Nations and the United States in 1951. Similar agreements followed that allowed UN stamps to be issued in Geneva, Switzerland, and in Vienna, Austria, which are home to other major UN offices.

UN stamps are renowned for their beautiful illustrations and innovative graphic designs, executed by some of the best artists and graphic designers in the world today. They depict the full range of issues which come before the Organization in fulfilling its global mandate, including environment, refugees, health, human rights, agriculture, outer space and the oceans, and technical assistance for development.

Since its creation, the United Nations has issued more than 1,000 stamps. They are highly regarded by knowledgeable international philatelists and stamp collectors of all ages. In fact, some 85 per cent of UN stamps are purchased by collectors. They are issued in only three currency denominations: US dollars, Swiss francs and Austrian schillings.

THE **UN** BOOKSHOP & GIFT CENTRE

The United Nations Gift Centre, Bookshop and Postal Administration Sales Counter are conveniently situated on the lower concourse level of the General Assembly Building. The Gift Centre offers an assortment of traditional souvenirs and artifacts from many lands. New York City residents and visitors alike enjoy it as a special place to find unique gifts and mementoes.

The Bookshop offers an extensive collection of UN publications on a rich variety of topics which generally focus on international issues of major concern to the United Nations family of organizations. Other attractive print products such as postcards, calendars, diaries, posters, flag charts and games with an international flavour are also available. United Nations postage stamps are available at the Postal Sales Counter. They can only be used at UN Headquarters in New York, the Palais des Nations in Geneva, Switzerland and the Vienna International Centre in Vienna, Austria.

HOW THE **UN** STORY IS **T**OLD

Greater cooperation among nations in recent years has resulted in increased use of the United Nations to resolve conflicts and to address long-standing challenges of economic and social development. As a result, the Organization, already a unique storehouse of knowledge and statistics, has become a vital source of current news and information and thus attracts a large media presence at UN Headquarters in New York and at its offices around the world.

The hundreds of newspaper, magazine, radio, photo and television journalists who are assigned to cover the UN "beat" are assisted by the Department of Public Information (DPI), whose media professionals generate press releases, books, pamphlets, radio and television programmes, periodicals, films, videos and photographs on the UN system's global activities. Other departments and UN bodies also carry out information programmes in their respective areas of expertise. The Organization also publishes a large selection of books, journals and statistical works – on topics ranging from international law and human rights to the environment, peace-keeping, trade, energy and economics – which are available at UN Headquarters and at bookstores throughout the world.

◀◀ *A large corps of photographers covers all aspects of the UN story, both at Headquarters and in the field.*

▼ *A video crew utilizes the backdrop of the Member States flags for a taped report by a television correspondent.*

One innovation in the DPI publishing programme is the "Blue Books" series, which captures for the first time in individual volumes the vital role the United Nations has played in peace-keeping and other major issues of concern to the international community.

All UN audio/visual and print products are widely disseminated in as many languages as possible. A network of more than 60 UN Information Centres in major cities throughout the world extends the outreach of the Organization. The ultimate aim of these efforts is to build awareness of the Organization's efforts and goals among the peoples of the world, and to enlist their support in fulfilling the purposes and ideals outlined in the Charter.

▶ *The UN Reproduction Section produces an enormous volume of printed materials, including conference and meetings documentation as well as many of the publications and information products generated at UN Headquarters. It can print materials in the six official UN languages, reproduce most photographic and cartographic work, and produce a variety of high-quality publications and other products. The Section operates on a 24-hour basis and, in 1994 alone, its staff produced 47,000 individual documents and publications.*

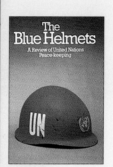

women

CHALLENGES

TO THE YEAR

2000

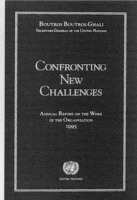

BOUTROS BOUTROS-GHALI

AGENDA POUR

LA PAIX

1995

DEUXIÈME ÉDITION
AUGMENTÉE DU SUPPLÉMENT
ET DE DOCUMENTS CONNEXES

BOUTROS BOUTROS-GHALI
SECRETARY-GENERAL OF THE UNITED NATIONS

CONFRONTING
NEW
CHALLENGES

ANNUAL REPORT ON THE WORK
OF THE ORGANIZATION
1995

UNITED NATIONS

The
Blue Helmets
A Review of United Nations
Peace-keeping

UN

The State of
WORLD
POPULATION   1995

UNFPA
United Nations
Population Fund

Dr. Nafis Sadik
Executive Director

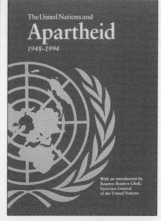

ABC
DES
NATIONS
UNIES

NATIONS UNIES

The United Nations and
Apartheid
1948–1994

With an introduction by
Boutros Boutros-Ghali,
Secretary-General
of the United Nations

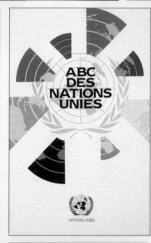

DECLARACIÓN
UNIVERSAL DE
DERECHOS HUMANOS

ADAPTACIÓN PARA NIÑOS DE RUTH ROCHA Y OCTAVIO ROTH

EDITORIAL
UNIVERSITARIA

NACIONES
UNIDAS

UNEP Reports and Proceedings Series, 7

WATER HYACINTH

Editor: G. Thyagarajan

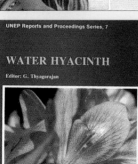

The Global Partnership
for Environment
and Development

A Guide to Agenda 21

UNITED NATIONS CONFERENCE ON TRADE AND DEVELOPMENT

TRADE AND DEVELOPMENT
REPORT, 1994

UNITED NATIONS

▶ *In the press briefing room at UN Headquarters, the Spokesman for the Secretary-General and an Associate Spokesperson (l. & r.) answer the questions of UN correspondents.*

▼ *Radio programmes on a vast range of subjects are produced at UN Headquarters and in the field for broadcast in multiple languages to a global audience.*

◀ *Through satellite communications technology, video coverage of proceedings and events at UN Headquarters is transmitted to UN Member States throughout the world.*

◀ *A large complex of radio
and television studios, film,
video and audio libraries and
a master control room are
located in the lower levels
of the General Assembly
Building. A technician is seen
here on the television
director's bridge monitoring
meetings coverage.*

OUR NEIGHBOURHOOD

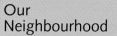
◄ *Demonstrators who wish to
bring their issues to the
attention of the international
community regularly use the
public forum of the streets.
This mass rally filled East 42nd
Street, a major crosstown
approach to the UN complex.*

◄ *Joggers are a common sight
at all hours of the day and
night as they enjoy broad,
treelined First Avenue along
the front of UN Headquarters.*

▼ *Native Americans attract
supporters to sign their petitions
during the International Year
of the World's Indigenous
People in 1993.*

UN OFFICES AROUND THE WORLD

The United Nations is
a global network of operations
that stretches far beyond the
Organization's Headquarters
in New York City.
Other important offices and
services include:

In Europe:
◀◀ *The Office of the United
Nations at Geneva,
Switzerland, the former
headquarters of the League
of Nations. Geneva is also
the home of the Economic
Commission for Europe and
a large number of UN
specialized agencies.*

◀ *The Vienna International
Centre in Vienna, Austria,
is headquarters of the
International Atomic Energy
Agency and the United
Nations Industrial
Development Organization.*

*In addition, the International
Court of Justice, one of the
main organs of the United
Nations, has its seat at
The Hague, Netherlands
(see chapter 6)*

In Africa*:*
*▸ The United Nations
Environment Programme
(UNEP) and the United
Nations Centre for Human
Settlements (HABITAT)
are both located in
Nairobi, Kenya.*

*◂ The United Nations Conference Centre
in Addis Ababa, Ethiopia, site of the
Economic Commission for Africa,
is shown here under construction.*

In Latin America:
▼ *The United Nations complex in Santiago, Chile, which houses the Economic Commission for Latin America and the Caribbean and the Latin American Institute for Economic and Social Planning.*

In Asia:
▲ *The United Nations Conference Centre in Bangkok, Thailand, site of the Economic and Social Commission for Asia and the Pacific.*

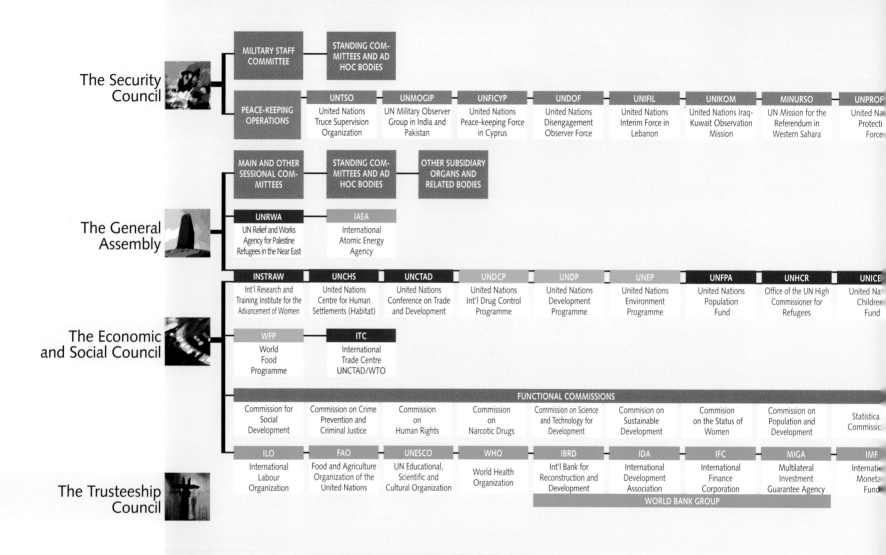

The Security Council

MILITARY STAFF COMMITTEE

STANDING COMMITTEES AND AD HOC BODIES

PEACE-KEEPING OPERATIONS

UNTSO	UNMOGIP	UNFICYP	UNDOF	UNIFIL	UNIKOM	MINURSO	UNPROF
United Nations Truce Supervision Organization	UN Military Observer Group in India and Pakistan	United Nations Peace-keeping Force in Cyprus	United Nations Disengagement Observer Force	United Nations Interim Force in Lebanon	United Nations Iraq-Kuwait Observation Mission	UN Mission for the Referendum in Western Sahara	United Na Protecti Force

The General Assembly

MAIN AND OTHER SESSIONAL COMMITTEES

STANDING COMMITTEES AND AD HOC BODIES

OTHER SUBSIDIARY ORGANS AND RELATED BODIES

UNRWA	IAEA
UN Relief and Works Agency for Palestine Refugees in the Near East	International Atomic Energy Agency

The Economic and Social Council

INSTRAW	UNCHS	UNCTAD	UNDCP	UNDP	UNEP	UNFPA	UNHCR	UNICE
Int'l Research and Training Institute for the Advancement of Women	United Nations Centre for Human Settlements (Habitat)	United Nations Conference on Trade and Development	United Nations Int'l Drug Control Programme	United Nations Development Programme	United Nations Environment Programme	United Nations Population Fund	Office of the UN High Commissioner for Refugees	United Na Childre Fund

WFP	ITC
World Food Programme	International Trade Centre UNCTAD/WTO

FUNCTIONAL COMMISSIONS

Commission for Social Development	Commission on Crime Prevention and Criminal Justice	Commission on Human Rights	Commission on Narcotic Drugs	Commission on Science and Technology for Development	Commision on Sustainable Development	Commision on the Status of Women	Commission on Population and Development	Statistica Commissio

ILO	FAO	UNESCO	WHO	IBRD	IDA	IFC	MIGA	IMF
International Labour Organization	Food and Agriculture Organization of the United Nations	UN Educational, Scientific and Cultural Organization	World Health Organization	Int'l Bank for Reconstruction and Development	International Development Association	International Finance Corporation	Multilateral Investment Guarantee Agency	Internati Moneta Fund

WORLD BANK GROUP

The Trusteeship Council

The International Court of Justice

The Secretariat

THE **UN** **S**YSTEM

UNOMIG	UNOMIL	UNMIH	UNAMIR	UNMOT	UNAVEM III	UNCRO	UNPREDEP
United Nations Observer Mission in Georgia	United Nations Observer Mission in Liberia	United Nations Mission in Haiti	United Nations Assistance Mission for Rwanda	United Nations Mission of Observers in Tajikistan	United Nations Angola Verification Mission III	United Nations Confidence Restoration Operation in Croatia	United Nations Preventive Deployment Force

UNIFEM	UNITAR	UNU	WFC
United Nations Development Fund for Women	United Nations Institute for Training and Research	United Nations University	World Food Council

REGIONAL COMMISSIONS					SESSIONAL AND STANDING COMMITTEES	EXPERT, AD HOC AND RELATED BODIES
Economic Commission for Africa (ECA)	Economic Commission for Europe (ECE)	Economic Commission for Latin America and the Caribbean (ECLAC)	Economic and Social Commission for Asia and the Pacific (ESCAP)	Economic and Social Commission for Western Asia (ESCWA)		

ICAO	UPU	ITU	WMO	IMO	WIPO	IFAD	UNIDO	WTO
International Civil Aviation Organization	Universal Postal Union	International Telecommunication Union	World Meteorological Organization	International Maritime Organization	World Intellectual Property Organization	International Fund for Agricultural Development	UN Industrial Development Organization	World Trade Organization*

▶ *United Nations organs (representative list only)*

▷ *United Nations programmes*

▶ *Specialized agencies and other autonomous organizations within the system*

▶ *Peace-keeping operations*

▶ *Other commissions, committees and ad hoc and related bodies*

* *Cooperative arrangements between the UN and the newly established WTO are currently under discussion.*

December 1995

PUBLISHED BY THE UNITED NATIONS **DEPARTMENT OF PUBLIC INFORMATION**
NEW YORK, NY 10017

UNITED NATIONS SALES NUMBER **E.97.I.8**
ISBN **92-1-100536-1**
DPI NUMBER **1744**
COPYRIGHT **© UNITED NATIONS 1995 AND 1997**
TEXTS **JAN RALPH**
DESIGN **LUIS SARDÁ**
PRINCIPAL PHOTOGRAPHY **ANDREA BRIZZI**
OTHER PHOTOGRAPHY *UNITED NATIONS PHOTO LIBRARY*
KEVIN BUBRISKI
DAVID BURNETT
LOIS CONNER
PETER CUMMINS
H.J.DAVIES
JIHAD EL HASSAN
L. GOODSMITH
MILTON GRANT
MARTHA GUTHRIE
ANNALIESE HOLLMANN
JOHN ISAAC
S. JACKSON
STEEN JOHANSEN
DAVID KINLEY
JEAN PIERRE LAFFONT
LARRY LUXNER
RUTH MASSEY
YUTAKA NAGATA
EVAN SCHNEIDER
PERNACCA SUDHAKARAN
MIKLOS TZOVARAS
RAY WITLIN
PHOTOGRAPH ON PAGE 2-6 *PAUL SKIPWORTH FOR EASTMAN KODAK COMPANY*

FOR INFORMATION ABOUT
UNITED NATIONS PUBLICATIONS
OF RELATED INTEREST CONTACT: **UNITED NATIONS PUBLICATIONS**
2 UNITED NATIONS PLAZA, ROOM DC2-853
NEW YORK, NY 10017 UNITED STATES OF AMERICA
TEL: (212) 963-8302 FAX: (212) 963-3489
(800) 255-9646

UNITED NATIONS PUBLICATIONS
SALES OFFICE AND BOOKSHOP
CH-1211 GENEVA 10
SWITZERLAND
TEL: 41(22) 917-26-13 FAX: 41(22) 917-00-27
41(22) 917-26-14

Visit the UN Home Page
on the Internet World Wide Web:

http://www.un.org/Publications

NOTE: DATA CURRENT AS OF JANUARY 1997